All Muslims
Shall Be Saved
by Elijah in the Bible

All Muslims Shall Be Saved

by *Elijah in the Bible*

BOOK # 2

To order additional copies of this book, contact:
Xlibris
1-888-795-4274
www.Xlibris.com
Orders@Xlibris.com

ISBN: Softcover   978-1-7960-9158-8
        EBook   978-1-7960-9159-5

Print information available on the last page

Rev. date: 02/29/2020

Why shouldest you do wrong when you know to do right.

Again I would say unto thee

I will not always chide with man

Heaven is forever & Hell is forever

so do good so you can live in heaven forever.

Hell is forever God wisheth thee not to go there.

I am a strict God I punish sin & reward righteousness.

Printed in the United States
By Bookmasters